Contents

Abbreviations

BXA	Bureau of Export Administration
CERT/CC	CERT Coordination Center
CIO	Chief Information Officer
EDA	Economic Development Administration
ESA	Economics and Statistics Administration
FedCIRC	Federal Computer Incident Response Center
ID	identification
IG	Inspector General
IT	information technology
ITA	International Trade Administration
MBDA	Minority Business Development Agency
NIST	National Institute of Standards and Technology
NTIA	National Telecommunications and Information Administration
OMB	Office of Management and Budget
O/S	Office of the Secretary

United States General Accounting Office
Washington, DC 20548

August 13, 2001

The Honorable W. J. "Billy" Tauzin
Chairman
Committee on Energy and Commerce
House of Representatives

Dear Mr. Chairman:

The Department of Commerce generates and disseminates some of the nation's most important economic information that is of paramount interest to U.S. businesses, policymakers, and researchers. Because the dramatic rise in the number and sophistication of cyberattacks on federal information systems is of growing concern, your committee requested that we determine if the Department of Commerce has effectively implemented (1) logical access and other information system controls over its computerized data,[1] (2) incident detection and response capabilities,[2] and (3) an information security management program and related procedures.

This report provides a general summary of the computer security weaknesses we identified in the unclassified information systems of the seven Commerce organizations we reviewed[3] as well as in the management of the department's information security program. Because of the sensitivity of specific weaknesses, we plan to issue a report designated for "Limited Official Use," which describes in more detail the

---

[1] Logical access controls are controls designed to protect computer resources from unauthorized modification, loss, or disclosure, specifically those controls that prevent or detect unauthorized access to sensitive data and programs that are stored or transmitted electronically.

[2] Incident detection is the process of identifying that an intrusion has been attempted, is occurring, or has occurred. Incident response is an action or series of actions constituting a reply or reaction against an attempted or successful intrusion.

[3] The Commerce organizations we reviewed were the Office of the Secretary, the Bureau of Export Administration, the Economic Development Administration, the Economics and Statistics Administration, the International Trade Administration, the Minority Business Development Agency, and the National Telecommunications and Information Administration. For the sake of simplification, throughout this report we use the term "bureaus" to refer to all seven of the Commerce organizations, although the Office of the Secretary is not actually a bureau. Appendix III provides a brief overview of these seven Commerce bureaus.

logical access control weaknesses identified and offers specific recommendations for correcting them.

We conducted penetration testing of sensitive Commerce systems from both inside Commerce headquarters and from a remote location through the Internet during a 2-month period. Using readily available software and common techniques, we attempted to penetrate systems and exploit identified control weaknesses to verify the vulnerability they presented. Appendix I contains further details on our objectives, scope, and methodology.

Results in Brief

Significant and pervasive computer security weaknesses place sensitive Department of Commerce systems [4] at risk. Individuals, both within and outside Commerce, could gain unauthorized access to these systems and thereby read, copy, modify, and delete sensitive economic, financial, personnel, and confidential business data. Moreover, intruders could disrupt the operations of systems that are critical to the mission of the department.

Inadequate logical access controls leave sensitive systems in the Commerce bureaus we reviewed highly susceptible to intrusions or disruptions. Specifically, we demonstrated that these bureaus had inadequate system access controls over user ID and password management, system administration functions, or critical systems and sensitive data files. Moreover, ineffectively secured configurations of the bureaus' operating systems exposed excessive system information to potential intruders and could undermine the continuous and reliable operation of important computer systems as well as allow users to bypass security controls. Furthermore, the Commerce bureaus did not have effective external or internal network security controls. In addition to logical access control issues, controls in other areas were inadequate. For example, the bureaus we reviewed did not properly segregate the computer duties of their staff to mitigate the risk of errors or fraud, and changes to software were not adequately controlled, which could adversely affect operations or the integrity of data. The bureaus also had not implemented adequate protection against the effects of potential

---

[4]By "sensitive" systems we refer to the systems that Commerce has defined as critical to the mission of the Department as well as systems that fit OMB Circular A-130, Appendix III, criteria for requiring special protection.

service disruptions. The vulnerabilities we identified were exacerbated by the extensive interconnectivity among Commerce systems, which allowed weaknesses in one bureau's systems to jeopardize the security of systems in other bureaus.

Poor detection and response capabilities at the Commerce bureaus we reviewed increase the likelihood that incidents of unauthorized access to sensitive systems will not be detected in time to prevent or minimize damage. Although we conducted extensive penetration testing of bureau networks during a 2-month period, the tested bureaus' general inability to notice our activities further demonstrates that they are not adequately monitoring events in their systems to identify and investigate signs of unusual or suspicious use.

The underlying cause for the numerous security weaknesses we discovered is that Commerce does not have an effective information security program in place to manage information security. As a result, the department is not adequately (1) identifying and assessing risks to determine needed security measures, (2) establishing and implementing policies and controls to meet those needs, (3) promoting awareness so that users understand the risks and the related policies and controls required to mitigate them, or (4) monitoring and evaluating established policies and controls to ensure that they continue to be both appropriate and effective.

At the time of our review, Commerce's Chief Information Officer (CIO), who was responsible for information security throughout the department, acknowledged that the information security program was ineffective, but believed that he had neither the authority nor adequate resources to effectively strengthen it. We are recommending that the Secretary of Commerce correct the information system security weaknesses we identified and establish a departmentwide information security program with the appropriate resources and authority to implement it.

In commenting on a draft of this report, the Secretary of Commerce concurred with our findings and said that Commerce is committed to improving the information security posture of the department. According to the Secretary, the heads of the Commerce bureaus have been directed to give priority to information security and to allocate sufficient resources to make sure that adequate security is in place. He added that the department has developed and is currently implementing action plans to correct the specific problems we identified.

Background

Information security is an important consideration for any organization that depends on information systems to carry out its mission. The dramatic expansion in computer interconnectivity and the exponential increase in the use of the Internet are changing the way our government, the nation, and much of the world communicate and conduct business. However, risks are significant, and they are growing. The number of computer security incidents reported to the CERT Coordination Center® (CERT/CC)[5] rose from 9,859 in 1999 to 21,756 in 2000. For the first six months of 2001, 15,476 incidents have been reported.

As the number of individuals with computer skills has increased, more intrusion or "hacking" tools have become readily available and relatively easy to use. A potential hacker can literally download tools from the Internet and "point and click" to start a hack. According to a recent National Institute of Standards and Technology (NIST) publication, hackers post 30 to 40 new tools to hacking sites on the Internet every month. The successful cyber attacks against such well-known U.S. e-commerce Internet sites as eBay, Amazon.com, and CNN.com by a 15-year old "script kiddie"[6] in February 2000 illustrate the risks. Without proper safeguards, these developments make it easier for individuals and groups with malicious intentions to gain unauthorized access to systems and use their access to obtain sensitive information, commit fraud, disrupt operations, or launch attacks against other organizations' sites.

Federal Systems Are at Risk

Government officials are increasingly concerned about federal computer systems, which process, store, and transmit enormous amounts of sensitive data and are indispensable to many federal operations. The federal government's systems are riddled with weaknesses that continue to put critical operations at risk. Since October 1998, the Federal Computer Incident Response Center's (FedCIRC)[7] records have shown an

---

[5]CERT Coordination Center® is a center of Internet security expertise located at the Software Engineering Institute, a federally funded research and development center operated by Carnegie Mellon University. CERT Coordination Center® is registered in the U.S. Patent and Trademark Office.

[6]The term "script kiddie" is used within the hacker community in a derogatory manner to refer to a hacker with little computer knowledge and few abilities who breaks into systems using scripts posted to the Internet by more skilled hackers.

[7]FedCIRC, a component of the General Service Administration's Technology Service, is the central coordinating activity for reporting security related incidents affecting computer systems within the federal government's civilian agencies and departments.

increasing trend in the number of attacks targeting government systems. In 1998 FedCIRC documented 376 incidents affecting 2,732 federal civilian systems and 86 military systems. In 2000, the number of attacks rose to 586 incidents affecting 575,568 federal systems and 148 of their military counterparts. Moreover, according to FedCIRC, these numbers reflect only reported incidents, which it estimates do not include as many as 80 percent of actual security incidents. According to FedCIRC, 155 of the incidents reported, which occurred at 32 agencies, resulted in what is known as a "root compromise."[8] For at least five of the root compromises, government officials were able to verify that access to sensitive information had been obtained.

How well federal agencies are addressing these risks is a topic of increasing interest in the executive and legislative branches. In January 2000, President Clinton issued a National Plan for Information Systems Protection[9] and designated computer security and critical infrastructure protection a priority management objective in his fiscal year 2001 budget. The new administration, federal agencies, and private industry have collaboratively begun to prepare a new version of the national plan that will outline an integrated approach to computer security and critical infrastructure protection.

The Congress, too, is increasingly interested in computer security, as evidenced by important hearings held during 1999, 2000, and 2001 on ways to strengthen information security practices throughout the federal government and on progress at specific agencies in addressing known vulnerabilities. Furthermore, in October 2000, the Congress included government information security reform provisions in the fiscal year 2001 National Defense Authorization Act. These provisions seek to ensure proper management and security for federal information systems by calling for agencies to adopt risk management practices that are consistent with those summarized in our 1998 Executive Guide.[10] The provisions also require annual agency program reviews and Inspector General (IG)

---

[8]A "root compromise" of a system gives the hacker the power to do anything that a systems administrator could do, from copying files to installing software such as "sniffer" programs that can monitor the activities of end users.

[9]*Defending America's Cyberspace: National Plan for Information Systems Protection: An Invitation to a Dialogue.*

[10]*Information Security Management: Learning From Leading Organizations* (GAO/AIMD-98-68, May 1998).

evaluations that must be reported to the Office of Management and Budget (OMB) as part of the budget process.

The federal CIO Council and others have also initiated several projects that are intended to promote and support security improvements to federal information systems. Over the past year, the CIO Council, working with NIST, OMB, and us, developed the Federal Information Technology Security Assessment Framework.[11] The framework provides agencies with a self-assessment methodology to determine the current status of their security programs and to establish targets for improvement. OMB has instructed agencies to use the framework to fulfill their annual assessment and reporting obligations.

Since 1996, our analyses of information security at major federal agencies have shown that systems are not being adequately protected. Our previous reports, and those of agency IGs, describe persistent computer security weaknesses that place a variety of critical federal operations at risk of inappropriate disclosures, fraud, and disruption.[12] This body of audit evidence has led us, since 1997, to designate computer security a governmentwide high-risk area.[13]

Our most recent summary analysis of federal information systems found that significant computer security weaknesses had been identified in 24 of the largest federal agencies, including Commerce.[14] During December 2000 and January 2001, Commerce's IG also reported significant computer security weaknesses in several of the department's bureaus and, in February 2001, reported information security as a material weakness affecting the department's ability to produce accurate data for financial statements.[15] The report stated that there were weaknesses in several areas, including entitywide security management, access controls,

---

[11] *Federal Information Technology Security Assessment Framework,* November 28, 2000.

[12] *Information Security: Serious Weaknesses Place Critical Federal Operations and Assets at Risk* (GAO/AIMD-98-92, September 23, 1998).

[13] *High-Risk Series: Information Management and Technology* (GAO/HR-97-9, February 1997), *High-Risk Series: An Update* (GAO/HR-99-1, January 1999), and *High-Risk Series: An Update* (GAO-01-263, January 2001).

[14] *Information Security: Serious and Widespread Weaknesses Persist at Federal Agencies* (GAO/AIMD-00-295, September 6, 2000).

[15] *Department of Commerce's Fiscal Year 2000 Consolidated Financial Statements,* Inspector General Audit Report No. FSD-12849-1-0001 (February 2001).

software change controls, segregation of duties, and service continuity planning. Moreover, a recent IG assessment of the department's information security program found fundamental weaknesses in the areas of policy and oversight.[16] Also, the IG designated information security as one of the top ten management challenges for the department.

Commerce Missions Are Diverse

Commerce's missions are among the most diverse of the federal government's cabinet departments, covering a wide range of responsibilities that include observing and managing natural resources and the environment; promoting commerce, regional development, and scientific research; and collecting, analyzing, and disseminating statistical information. Commerce employs about 40,000 people in 14 operating bureaus with numerous offices in the U.S. and overseas, each pursuing disparate programs and activities.

Information technology (IT) is a critical tool for Commerce to support these missions. The department spends significant resources—reportedly over $1.5 billion in fiscal year 2000—on IT systems and services. As a percentage of total agency expenditures on IT, Commerce ranks among the top agencies in the federal government, with 17 percent of its $9-billion fiscal year 2000 budget reported as spent on IT.

A primary mission of Commerce is to promote job creation and improved living standards for all Americans by furthering U.S. economic growth, and the seven bureaus we reviewed support this mission through a wide array of programs and services. Commerce uses IT to generate and disseminate some of the nation's most important economic information. The International Trade Administration (ITA) promotes the export of U.S. goods and services—which amounted to approximately $1.1 trillion in fiscal year 2000. Millions of American jobs depend on exports, and with 96 percent of the world's consumers living outside U.S. borders, international trade is increasingly important to supporting this mission. The Economics and Statistics Administration (ESA) develops, prepares, analyzes, and disseminates important indicators of the U.S. that present basic information on such key issues as economic growth, regional development, and the U.S. role in the world economy. This information is of paramount interest to researchers, business, and policymakers.

---

[16] *Office of the Chief Information Officer: Additional Focus Needed on Information Technology Security Policy and Oversight* (Inspection Report No. OSE-13573/March 2001).

The Bureau of Export Administration (BXA), whose efforts supported sales of approximately $4.2 billion in fiscal year 1999, assists in stimulating the growth of U.S. exports while protecting national security interests by helping to stop the proliferation of weapons of mass destruction. Sensitive data such as that relating to national security, nuclear proliferation, missile technology, and chemical and biological warfare reside in this bureau's systems.

Commerce's ability to fulfill its mission depends on the confidentiality, integrity, and availability of this sensitive information. For example, export data residing in the BXA systems reflect technologies that have both civil and military applications; the misuse, modification, or deletion of these data could threaten our national security or public safety and affect foreign policy. Much of these data are also business proprietary. If it were compromised, the business could not only lose its market share, but dangerous technologies might end up in the hands of renegade nations who threaten our national security or that of other nations.

Commerce's IT Infrastructure Is Decentralized

Commerce's IT infrastructure is decentralized. Although the Commerce IT Review Board approves major acquisitions, most bureaus have their own IT budgets and act independently to acquire, develop, operate, and maintain their own infrastructure. For example, Commerce has 14 different data centers, diverse hardware platforms and software environments, and 20 independently managed e-mail systems. The bureaus also develop and control their own individual networks to serve their specific needs. These networks vary greatly in size and complexity. For example, one bureau has as many as 155 local area networks and 3,000 users spread over 50 states and 80 countries. Some of these networks are owned, operated, and managed by individual programs within the same bureau.

Because Commerce does not have a single, departmentwide common network infrastructure to facilitate data communications across the department, the bureaus have established their own access paths to the Internet, which they rely on to communicate with one another. In April 2001, the department awarded a contract for a $4 million project to consolidate the individual bureaus' local area networks within its headquarters building onto a common network infrastructure. However, until this project is completed, each of the bureaus is expected to continue to configure, operate, and maintain its own unique networks.

Improvements to Information Security Have Been Initiated

Recognizing the importance of its data and operations, in September 1993 Commerce established departmentwide information security policies that defined and assigned a full set of security responsibilities, ranging from the department level down to individual system owners and users within the bureaus. Since 1998, the Commerce CIO position has been responsible for developing and implementing the department's information security program. An information security manager, under the direction of the CIO's Office of Information Policy, Planning, and Review, is tasked with carrying out the responsibilities of the program. The CIO's responsibilities for the security of classified systems have been delegated to the Office of Security.

In the last 2 years, the CIO introduced several initiatives that are essential to improving the security posture of the department. After a 1999 contracted evaluation of the bureaus' security plans determined that 43 percent of Commerce's most critical assets did not have current information system security plans, the CIO issued a memorandum calling for the bureaus to prepare security plans that comply with federal regulations. Also, in May 2000, the Office of the CIO performed a summary evaluation of the status of all the bureaus' information security based on the bureaus' own self-assessments. The results determined that overall information security program compliance was minimal, that no formal information security awareness and training programs were provided by the bureaus, and that incident response capabilities were either absent or informal. The Commerce IG indicated that subsequent meetings between the Office of the CIO and the bureaus led to improvements. The Office of the CIO plans to conduct another evaluation this year and, based on a comparison with last year's results, measure the bureaus' success in strengthening their security postures.

Finally, for the past year, the CIO attempted to restructure the department's IT management to increase his span of control over information security within the bureaus by enforcing his oversight authority and involvement in budgeting for IT resources. The CIO resigned in May 2001 and, in June 2001, after completion of our fieldwork, the Secretary of Commerce approved a high-level IT restructuring plan. The acting CIO stated that Commerce is developing a more detailed implementation plan.

Logical Access Controls Were Inadequate

A basic management objective for any organization is the protection of its information systems and critical data from unauthorized access. Organizations accomplish this objective by establishing controls that limit access to only authorized users, effectively configuring their operating systems, and securely implementing networks. However, our tests identified weaknesses in each of these control areas in all of the Commerce bureaus we reviewed. We demonstrated that individuals, both external and internal to Commerce, could compromise security controls to gain extensive unauthorized access to Commerce networks and systems. These weaknesses place the bureaus' information systems at risk of unauthorized access, which could lead to the improper disclosure, modification, or deletion of sensitive information and the disruption of critical operations. As previously noted, because of the sensitivity of specific weaknesses, we plan to issue a report designated for "Limited Official Use," which describes in more detail each of the computer security weaknesses identified and offers specific recommendations for correcting them.

System Access Controls Were Weak

Effective system access controls provide mechanisms that require users to identify themselves and authenticate[17] their identity, limit the use of system administrator capabilities to authorized individuals, and protect sensitive system and data files. As with many organizations, passwords are Commerce's primary means of authenticating user identity. Because system administrator capabilities provide the ability to read, modify, or delete any data or files on the system and modify the operating system to create access paths into the system, such capabilities should be limited to the minimum access levels necessary for systems personnel to perform their duties. Also, information can be protected by using controls that limit an individual's ability to read, modify, or delete information stored in sensitive system files.

User ID and Password Management Controls Were Not Effective

One of the primary methods to prevent unauthorized access to information system resources is through effective management of user IDs and passwords. To accomplish this objective, organizations should establish controls that include requirements to ensure that well-chosen passwords are required for user authentication, passwords are changed periodically, the number of invalid password attempts is limited to preclude password

---

[17]Authenticating is the process of verifying that a user is allowed to access a system or an account.

guessing, and the confidentiality of passwords is maintained and protected.

All Commerce bureaus reviewed were not effectively managing user IDs and passwords to sufficiently reduce the risk that intruders could gain unauthorized access to its information systems to (1) change system access and other rules, (2) potentially read, modify, and delete or redirect network traffic, and (3) read, modify, and delete sensitive information. Specifically, systems were either not configured to require passwords or, if passwords were required, they were relatively easy to guess. For example,

- powerful system administrator accounts did not require passwords, allowing anyone who could connect to certain systems through the network to log on as a system administrator without having to use a password,
- systems allowed users to change their passwords to a blank password, completely circumventing the password control function,
- passwords were easily guessed words, such as "password,"
- passwords were the same as the user's ID, and
- commonly known default passwords set by vendors when systems were originally shipped had never been changed.

Although frequent password changes reduce the risk of continued unauthorized use of a compromised password, systems in four of the bureaus reviewed had a significant number of passwords that never required changing or did not have to be changed for 273 years. Also, systems in six of the seven bureaus did not limit the number of times an individual could try to log on to a user ID. Unlimited attempts allow intruders to keep trying passwords until a correct password is discovered.

Further, all Commerce bureaus reviewed did not adequately protect the passwords of their system users through measures such as encryption, as illustrated by the following examples:

- User passwords were stored in readable text files that could be viewed by all users on one bureau's systems.
- Files that store user passwords were not protected from being copied by intruders, who could then take the copied password files and decrypt user passwords. The decrypted passwords could then be used to gain unauthorized access to systems by intruders masquerading as legitimate users.
- Over 150 users of one system could read the unencrypted password of a powerful system administrator's account.

Control of System Administration Functions Was Not Adequate

System administrators perform important functions in support of the operations of computer systems. These functions include defining security controls, granting users access privileges, changing operating system configurations, and monitoring system activity. In order to perform these functions, system administrators have powerful privileges that enable them to manipulate operating system and security controls. Privileges to perform these system administration functions should be granted only to employees who require such privileges to perform their responsibilities and who are specifically trained to understand and exercise those privileges. Moreover, the level of privilege granted to employees should not exceed the level required for them to perform their assigned duties. Finally, systems should provide accountability for the actions of system administrators on the systems.

However, Commerce bureaus granted the use of excessive system administration privileges to employees who did not require such privileges to perform their responsibilities and who were not trained to exercise them. For example, a very powerful system administration privilege that should be used only in exceptional circumstances, such as recovery from a power failure, was granted to 20 individuals. These 20 individuals had the ability to access all of the information stored on the system, change important system configurations that could affect the system's reliability, and run any program on the computer. Further, Commerce management also acknowledged that not all staff with access to this administrative privilege had been adequately trained.

On other important systems in all seven bureaus, system administrators were sharing user IDs and passwords so that systems could not provide an audit trail of access by system administrators, thereby limiting accountability. By not effectively controlling the number of staff who exercise system administrator privileges, restricting the level of such privileges granted to those required to perform assigned duties, or ensuring that only well-trained staff have these privileges, Commerce is increasing the risk that unauthorized activity could occur and the security of sensitive information could be compromised.

Access to Critical Systems and Sensitive Data Files Was Not Adequately Restricted

Access privileges to individual critical systems and sensitive data files should be restricted to authorized users. Not only does this restriction protect files that may contain sensitive information from unauthorized access, but it also provides another layer of protection against intruders who may have successfully penetrated one system from significantly extending their unauthorized access and activities to other systems. Examples of access privileges are the capabilities to read, modify, or delete a file. Privileges can be granted to individual users, to groups of users, or to everyone who accesses the system.

Six of the seven bureaus' systems were not configured to appropriately restrict access to sensitive system and/or data files. For example, critical system files could be modified by all users to allow them to bypass security controls. Also, excessive access privileges to sensitive data files such as export license applications were granted. Systems configured with excessive file access privileges are extremely vulnerable to compromise because such configurations could enable an intruder to read, modify, or delete sensitive system and data files, or to disrupt the availability and integrity of the system.

Operating Systems Were Ineffectively Secured

Operating system controls are essential to ensure that the computer systems and security controls function as intended. Operating systems are relied on by all the software and hardware in a computer system. Additionally, all users depend on the proper operation of the operating system to provide a consistent and reliable processing environment, which is essential to the availability and reliability of the information stored and processed by the system.

Operating system controls should limit the extent of information that systems provide to facilitate system interconnectivity. Operating systems should be configured to help ensure that systems are available and that information stored and processed is not corrupted. Controls should also limit the functions[18] of the computer system to prevent insecure system configurations or the existence of functions not needed to support the operations of the system. If functions are not properly controlled, they can be used by intruders to circumvent security controls.

Excessive System Information Was Exposed

To facilitate interconnectivity between computer systems, operating systems are configured to provide descriptive and technical information, such as version numbers and system names, to other computer systems and individuals when connections are being established. At the same time,

---

[18]Operating system functions are capabilities added to the operating system to support specific processing requirements necessary for the system to perform its intended purpose. Examples of operating system functions include the capability to receive electronic mail, have technical support performed remotely, transfer data between different types of computer systems, and have users safely execute powerful programs without granting those users powerful access privileges.

however, systems should be configured to limit the amount of information that is made available to other systems and unidentified individuals because this information can be misused by potential intruders to learn the characteristics and vulnerabilities of that system to assist in intrusions.

Systems in all bureaus reviewed were not configured to control excessive system information from exposure to potential attackers. The configuration of Commerce systems provided excessive amounts of information to anyone, including external users, without the need for authentication. Our testing demonstrated that potential attackers could collect information about systems, such as computer names, types of operating systems, functions, version numbers, user information, and other information that could be useful to circumvent security controls and gain unauthorized access.

Operating Systems Were Poorly Configured

The proper configuration of operating systems is important to ensuring the reliable operation of computers and the continuous availability and integrity of critical information. Operating systems should be configured so that the security controls throughout the system function effectively and the system can be depended on to support the organization's mission.

Commerce bureaus did not properly configure operating systems to ensure that systems would be available to support bureau missions or prevent the corruption of the information relied on by management and the public. For example, in a large computer system affecting several bureaus, there were thousands of important programs that had not been assigned unique names. In some instances, as many as six different programs all shared the same name, many of which were different versions of the same program. Although typically the complexity of such a system may require the installation of some programs that are identically named and authorized programs must be able to bypass security in order to operate, there was an excessive number of such programs installed on this system, many of which were capable of bypassing security controls. Because these different programs are identically named, unintended programs could be inadvertently run, potentially resulting in the corruption of data or disruption of system operations. Also, because these powerful programs are duplicated, there is an increased likelihood that they could be misused to bypass security controls.

In this same system, critical parts of the operating system were shared by the test and production systems used to process U.S. export information. Because critical parts were shared, as changes are made in the test system, these changes could also affect the production system. Consequently, changes could be made in the test system that would cause the production system to stop operating normally and shut down. Changes in the test system could also cause important Commerce data in the production system to become corrupted. Commerce management acknowledged that the isolation between these two systems needed to be strengthened to mitigate these risks.

Systems Had Unnecessary and Poorly Configured Functions

Operating system functions should be limited to support only the capabilities needed by each specific computer system. Moreover, these functions should be appropriately configured. Unnecessary operating system functions can be used to gain unauthorized access to a system and target that system for a denial-of-service attack.[19] Poorly configured operating system functions can allow individuals to bypass security controls and access sensitive information without requiring proper identification and authentication.

Unnecessary and poorly configured system functions existed on important computer systems in all the bureaus we reviewed.[20] For example, unnecessary functions allowed us to gain access to a system from the Internet. Through such access and other identified weaknesses, we were able to gain system administration privileges on that system and subsequently gain access to other systems within other Commerce bureaus. Also, poorly configured functions would have allowed users to bypass security controls and gain unrestricted access to all programs and data.

Network Security Was Ineffective

Networks are a series of interconnected IT devices and software that allow groups of individuals to share data, printers, communications systems, electronic mail, and other resources. They provide the entry point for access to electronic information assets and provide users with access

---

[19]A denial-of-service attack is an attack in which one user takes up so much of a shared resource that none of the resources is left for other users. Denial-of-service attacks compromise the availability of the resources. There are two types of denial-of-service attacks. The first type of attack attempts to damage or destroy resources so that you cannot use them. The second type of attack overloads some system service or exhausts some resource, thus preventing others from using that service.

[20]Because of the sensitivity of this information, specific vulnerabilities are not discussed in this report. However, the report designated for "Limited Official Use" will describe in more detail the vulnerable functions we identified and offer specific recommendations for correcting them.

to the information technologies they need to satisfy the organization's mission. Controls should restrict access to networks from sources external to the network. Controls should also limit the use of systems from sources internal to the network to authorized users for authorized purposes.

External threats include individuals outside an organization attempting to gain unauthorized access to an organization's networks using the Internet, other networks, or dial-up modems. Another form of external threat is flooding a network with large volumes of access requests so that the network is unable to respond to legitimate requests, one type of denial-of-service attack. External threats can be countered by implementing security controls on the perimeters of the network, such as firewalls,[21] that limit user access and data interchange between systems and users within the organization's network and systems and users outside the network, especially on the Internet. An example of perimeter defenses is only allowing pre-approved computer systems from outside the network to exchange certain types of data with computer systems inside the network. External network controls should guard the perimeter of the network from connections with other systems and access by individuals who are not authorized to connect with and use the network.

Internal threats come from sources that are within an organization's networks, such as a disgruntled employee with access privileges who attempts to perform unauthorized activities. Also, an intruder who has successfully penetrated a network's perimeter defenses becomes an internal threat when the intruder attempts to compromise other parts of an organization's network security as a result of gaining access to one system within the network. For example, at Commerce, users of one bureau who have no business need to access export license information on another bureau's network should not have had network connections to that system. External network security controls should prevent unauthorized access from outside threats, but if those controls fail, internal network security controls should also prevent the intruder from gaining unauthorized access to other computer systems within the network.

---

[21]Firewalls are hardware and software components that protect one set of system resources (e.g., computers and networks) from attack by outside network users (e.g., Internet users) by blocking and checking all incoming network traffic. Firewalls permit authorized users to access and transmit privileged information and deny access to unauthorized users.

None of the Commerce bureaus reviewed had effective external and internal network security controls. Individuals, both within and outside Commerce, could compromise external and internal security controls to gain extensive unauthorized access to Commerce networks and systems. Bureaus employed a series of external control devices, such as firewalls, in some, but not all, of the access paths to their networks. However, these controls did not effectively prevent unauthorized access to Commerce networks from the Internet or through poorly controlled dial-up modems that bypass external controls. For example, four bureaus had not configured their firewalls to adequately protect their information systems from intruders on the Internet. Also, six dial-up modems were installed so that anyone could connect to their network without having to use a password, thereby circumventing the security controls provided by existing firewalls.

Our testing demonstrated that, once access was gained by an unauthorized user on the Internet or through a dial-up modem to one bureau's networks, that intruder could circumvent ineffective internal network controls to gain unauthorized access to other, connected networks within Commerce. Such weak internal network controls could allow an unauthorized intruder or authorized user on one bureau's network to change the configuration of other bureaus' network controls so that the user could observe network traffic, including passwords and sensitive information that Commerce transmits in readable clear text, and disrupt network operations.

The external and internal security controls of the different Commerce bureau networks did not provide a consistent level of security in part because bureaus independently configured and operated their networks as their own individual networks. For example, four of the bureaus we reviewed had their own independently controlled access points to the Internet.

Because the different bureaus' networks are actually logically interconnected and perform as one large interconnected network, the ineffective network security controls of one bureau jeopardize the security of other bureaus' networks. Weaknesses in the external and internal network controls of the individual bureaus heighten the risk that outside intruders with no prior knowledge of bureau user IDs or passwords, as well as Commerce employees with malicious intent, could exploit the other security weaknesses in access and operating system controls discussed above to misuse, improperly disclose, or destroy sensitive information.

Other Information System Controls Were Not Adequate

In addition to logical access controls, other important controls should be in place to ensure the confidentiality, integrity, and availability of an organization's data. These information system controls include policies, procedures, and techniques to provide appropriate segregation of duties among computer personnel, prevent unauthorized changes to application programs, and ensure the continuation of computer processing operations in case of unexpected interruption. The Commerce bureaus had weaknesses in each of these areas that heightened the risks already created by their lack of effective access controls.

Computer Duties Were Not Properly Segregated

A fundamental technique for safeguarding programs and data is to segregate the duties and responsibilities of computer personnel to reduce the risk that errors or fraud will occur and go undetected. OMB A-130, Appendix III, requires that roles and responsibilities be divided so that a single individual cannot subvert a critical process. Once policies and job descriptions that support the principles of segregation of duties have been established, access controls can then be implemented to ensure that employees perform only compatible functions.

None of the seven bureaus in our review had specific policies documented to identify and segregate incompatible duties, and bureaus had assigned incompatible duties to staff. For example, staff were performing incompatible computer operations and security duties. In another instance, the bureau's security officer had the dual role of also being the bureau's network administrator. These two functions are not compatible since the individual's familiarity with system security could then allow him or her to bypass security controls either to facilitate performing administrative duties or for malicious purposes.

Furthermore, none of the bureaus reviewed had implemented processes and procedures to mitigate the increased risks of personnel with incompatible duties. Specifically, none of the bureaus had a monitoring process to ensure appropriate segregation of duties, and management did not review access activity. Until Commerce restricts individuals from performing incompatible duties and implements compensating access controls, such as supervision and review, Commerce's sensitive information will face increased risks of improper disclosure, inadvertent or deliberate misuse, and deletion, all of which could occur without detection.

Software Changes Were Not Adequately Controlled

Also important for an organization's information security is ensuring that only authorized and fully tested software is placed in operation. To make certain that software changes are needed, work as intended, and do not result in the loss of data and program integrity, such changes should be documented, authorized, tested, and independently reviewed. Federal guidelines emphasize the importance of establishing controls to monitor the installation of and changes to software to ensure that software functions as expected and that a historical record is maintained of all changes.[22]

We have previously reported on Commerce's lack of policies on software change controls.[23] Specific key controls not addressed were (1) operating system software changes, monitoring, and access and (2) controls over application software libraries including access to code, movement of software programs, and inventories of software. Moreover, implementation was delegated to the individual bureaus, which had not established written policies or procedures for managing software changes.

Only three of the seven bureaus we reviewed mentioned software change controls in their system security plans, while none of the bureaus had policies or procedures for controlling the installation of software. Such policies are important to ensure that software changes do not adversely affect operations or the integrity of the data on the system. Without proper software change controls, there are risks that security features could be inadvertently or deliberately omitted or rendered inoperable, processing irregularities could occur, or malicious code could be introduced.

Service Continuity Planning Was Incomplete

Organizations must take steps to ensure that they are adequately prepared to cope with a loss of operational capability due to earthquakes, fires, sabotage, or other disruptions. An essential element in preparing for such catastrophes is an up-to-date, detailed, and fully tested recovery plan that covers all key computer operations. Such a plan is critical for helping to ensure that information system operations and data can be promptly restored in the event of a service disruption. OMB Circular A-130, Appendix III, requires that agency security plans assure that there is an

---

[22]NIST Special Publication 800-18: *Guide for Developing Security Plans for Information Technology Systems,* December 1998.

[23]*Software Change Controls at Commerce* (GAO/AIMD-00-187R, June 30, 2000).

ability to restore service sufficient to meet the minimal needs of users. Commerce policy also requires a backup or alternate operations strategy.

The Commerce bureaus we reviewed had not developed comprehensive plans to ensure the continuity of service in the event of a service disruption. Described below are examples of service continuity weaknesses we identified at the seven Commerce bureaus.

- None of the seven bureaus had completed recovery plans for all their sensitive systems.
- Although one bureau had developed two recovery plans, one for its data center and another for its software development installation center, the bureau did not have plans to cover disruptions to the rest of its critical systems, including its local area network.
- Systems at six of the seven bureaus did not have documented backup procedures.
- One bureau stated that it had an agreement with another Commerce bureau to back it up in case of disruptions; however, this agreement had not been documented.
- One bureau stated in its backup strategy that tapes used for system recovery are neither stored off-site nor protected from destruction. For example, backup for its network file servers is kept in a file cabinet in a bureau official's supply room, and backup tapes for a database and web server are kept on the shelf above the server. In case of a destructive event, the backups could be subject to the same damage as the primary files.
- Two bureaus had no backup facilities for key network devices such as firewalls.

Until each of the Commerce bureaus develops and fully tests comprehensive recovery plans for all of its sensitive systems, there is little assurance that in the event of service interruptions, many functions of the organization will not effectively cease and critical data will be lost.

Poor Incident Detection and Response Capabilities Further Impair Security

As our government becomes increasingly dependent on information systems to support sensitive data and mission-critical operations, it is essential that agencies protect these resources from misuse and disruption. An important component of such protective efforts is the capability to promptly identify and respond to incidents of attempted system intrusions. Agencies can better protect their information systems from intruders by developing formalized mechanisms that integrate incident handling functions with the rest of the organizational security infrastructure. Through such mechanisms, agencies can address how to (1) prevent intrusions before they occur, (2) detect intrusions as they occur, (3) respond to successful intrusions, and (4) report intrusions to staff and management.

Although essential to protecting resources, Commerce bureau incident handling capabilities are inadequate in preventing, detecting, responding to, and reporting incidents. Because the bureaus have not implemented comprehensive and consistent incident handling capabilities, decision-making may be haphazard when a suspected incident is detected, thereby impairing responses and reporting. Thus, there is little assurance that unauthorized attempts to access sensitive information will be identified and appropriate actions taken in time to prevent or minimize damage. Until adequate incident detection and response capabilities are established, there is a greater risk that intruders could be successful in copying, modifying, or deleting sensitive data and disrupting essential operations.

Incident Handling Mechanisms Have Not Been Established or Implemented

Accounting for and analyzing computer security incidents are effective ways for organizations to better understand threats to their information systems. Such analyses can also pinpoint vulnerabilities that need to be addressed so that they will not be exploited again. OMB Circular A-130, Appendix III, requires agencies to establish formal incident response mechanisms dedicated to evaluating and responding to security incidents in a manner that protects their own information and helps to protect the information of others who might be affected by the incident. These formal incident response mechanisms should also share information concerning common vulnerabilities and threats within the organization as well as with other organizations. By establishing such mechanisms, agencies help to ensure that they can more effectively coordinate their activities when incidents occur.

Although the Commerce CIO issued a July 1999 memorandum to all bureau CIOs outlining how to prevent, detect, respond to, and report incidents, the guidance has been inconsistently implemented. Six of the seven bureaus we reviewed have only ad hoc processes and procedures for handling incidents. None have established and implemented all of the requirements of the memo. Furthermore, Commerce does not have a centralized function to coordinate the handling of incidents on a departmentwide basis.

Incidents Could Be Prevented

Two preventive measures for deterring system intrusions are to install (1) software updates to correct known vulnerabilities and (2) messages warning intruders that their activities are punishable by law. First, federal guidance, industry advisories, and best practices all stress the importance of installing updated versions of operating systems and the software that supports system operations to protect against vulnerabilities that have been discovered in previously released versions. If new versions have not yet been released, "patches" that fix known flaws are often readily available and should be installed in the interim. Updating operating systems and other software to correct these vulnerabilities is important because once vulnerabilities are discovered, technically sophisticated hackers write scripts to exploit them and often post these scripts to the Internet for the widespread use of lesser skilled hackers. Since these scripts are easy to use, many security breaches happen when intruders take advantage of vulnerabilities for which patches are available but system administrators have not applied the patches. Second, Public Law 99-74 requires that a warning message be displayed upon access to all federal computer systems notifying users that unauthorized use is punishable by fines and imprisonment. Not only does the absence of a warning message fail to deter potential intruders, but, according to the law, pursuing and prosecuting intruders is more difficult if they have not been previously made fully aware of the consequences of their actions.

Commerce has not fully instituted these two key measures to prevent incidents. First, many bureau systems do not have system software that has been updated to address known security exposures. For example, during our review, we discovered 20 systems with known vulnerabilities for which patches were available but not installed. Moreover, all the bureaus we reviewed were still running older versions of software used on critical control devices that manage network connections. Newer versions of software are available that correct the known security flaws of the versions that were installed. Second, in performing our testing of network security, we observed that warning messages had not been installed for several network paths into Commerce systems that we tested.

Incident Detection Capabilities Have Not Been Implemented

Even though strong controls may not block all intrusions, organizations can reduce the risks associated with such events if they take steps to detect intrusions and the consequent misuse before significant damage can be done. Federal guidance emphasizes the importance of using detection systems to protect systems from the threats associated with increasing network connectivity and reliance on information systems. Additionally, federally funded activities, such as CERT/CC, the Department of Energy's Computer Incident Advisory Capability, and FedCIRC are available to assist organizations in detecting and responding to incidents.

Although the CIO's July memo directs Commerce bureaus to monitor their information systems to detect unusual or suspicious activities, all the bureaus we reviewed were either not using monitoring programs or had only partially implemented their capabilities. For example, only two of the bureaus had installed intrusion detection systems. Also, system and network logs frequently had not been activated or were not reviewed to detect possible unauthorized activity. Moreover, modifications to critical operating system components were not logged, and security reports detailing access to sensitive data and resources were not sent to data owners for their review.

The fact that bureaus we reviewed detected our activities only four times during the 2 months that we performed extensive external testing of Commerce networks, which included probing over 1,000 system devices, indicates that, for the most part, they are unaware of intrusions. For example, although we spent several weeks probing one bureau's networks and obtained access to many of its systems, our activities were never detected. Moreover, during testing we identified evidence of hacker activity that Commerce had not previously detected. Without monitoring their information systems, the bureaus cannot

- know how, when, and who performs specific computer activities,
- be aware of repeated attempts to bypass security, or
- detect suspicious patterns of behavior such as two users with the same ID and password logged on simultaneously or users with system administrator privileges logged on at an unexpected time of the day or night.

As a result, the bureaus have little assurance that potential intrusions will be detected in time to prevent or, at least, minimize damage.

Incident Response Procedures Have Not Been Established

The CIO's July memo also outlines how the bureaus are to respond to detected incidents. Instructions include responses such as notifying appropriate officials, deploying an on-site team to survey the situation, and isolating the attack to learn how it was executed.

Only one of the seven bureaus reviewed has documented response procedures. Consequently, we experienced inconsistent responses when our testing was detected. For example, one bureau responded to our scanning of their systems by scanning ours in return.[24] In another bureau, a Commerce employee who detected our testing responded by launching a software attack against our systems. In neither case was bureau management previously consulted or informed of these responses.

The lack of documented incident response procedures increases the risk of inappropriate responses. For example, employees could

- take no action,
- take insufficient actions that fail to limit potential damage,
- take overzealous actions that unnecessarily disrupt critical operations, or
- take actions, such as launching a retaliatory attack, that could be considered improper.

Bureaus Have Not Been Reporting Incidents

The CIO's July memo specifically requires bureau employees who suspect an incident or violation to contact their supervisor and the bureau security officer, who should report the incident to the department's information security manager. Reporting detected incidents is important because this information provides valuable input for risk assessments, helps in prioritizing security improvement efforts, and demonstrates trends of threats to an organization as a whole.

The bureaus we reviewed have not been reporting all detected incidents. During our 2-month testing period, 16 incidents were reported by the seven bureaus collectively, 10 of which were generated to report computer viruses. Four of the other six reported incidents related to our testing activities, one of which was reported after our discovery of evidence of a successful intrusion that Commerce had not previously detected and reported. However, we observed instances of detected incidents that were not reported to bureau security officers or the department's information

---

[24]Scanning is a favorite approach of computer hackers to discover what computer network services a computer provides so that it can be probed for vulnerabilities.

security manager. For example, the Commerce employees who responded to our testing by targeting our systems in the two instances discussed above did not report either of the two incidents to their own bureau's security officer.

By not reporting incidents, the bureaus lack assurance that identified security problems have been tracked and eliminated and the targeted system restored and validated. Furthermore, information about incidents could be valuable to other bureaus and assist the department as a whole to recognize and secure systems against general patterns of intrusion.

Commerce Does Not Have an Effective Information Security Management Program

The underlying cause for the numerous weaknesses we identified in bureau information system controls is that Commerce does not have an effective departmentwide information security management program in place to ensure that sensitive data and critical operations receive adequate attention and that the appropriate security controls are implemented to protect them. Our study of security management best practices, as summarized in our 1998 Executive Guide,[25] found that leading organizations manage their information security risks through an ongoing cycle of risk management. This management process involves (1) establishing a centralized management function to coordinate the continuous cycle of activities while providing guidance and oversight for the security of the organization as a whole, (2) identifying and assessing risks to determine what security measures are needed, (3) establishing and implementing policies and procedures that meet those needs, (4) promoting security awareness so that users understand the risks and the related policies and procedures in place to mitigate those risks, and (5) instituting an ongoing monitoring program of tests and evaluations to ensure that policies and procedures are appropriate and effective. However, Commerce's information security management program is not effective in any of these key elements.

Centralized Management Is Weak

Establishing a central management function is the starting point of the information security management cycle mentioned above. This function provides knowledge and expertise on information security and coordinates organizationwide security-related activities associated with

---

[25]*Information Security Management: Learning From Leading Organizations* (GAO/AIMD-98-68, May 1998).

the other four segments of the risk management cycle. For example, the function researches potential threats and vulnerabilities, develops and adjusts organizationwide policies and guidance, educates users about current information security risks and the policies in place to mitigate those risks, and provides oversight to review compliance with policies and to test the effectiveness of controls. This central management function is especially important to managing the increased risks associated with a highly connected computing environment. By providing coordination and oversight of information security activities organizationwide, such a function can help ensure that weaknesses in one unit's systems do not place the entire organization's information assets at undue risk.

According to Commerce policy, broad program responsibility for information security throughout the department is assigned to the CIO. Department of Commerce Organization Order 15-23 of July 5, 2000, specifically tasks the CIO with developing and implementing the department's information security program to ensure the confidentiality, integrity, and availability of information and IT resources. These responsibilities include developing policies, procedures, and directives for information security; providing mandatory periodic training in computer security awareness and accepted practice; and identifying and developing security plans for Commerce systems that contain sensitive information. Furthermore, the CIO is also formally charged with carrying out the Secretary's responsibilities for computer security under OMB Circular A-130, Appendix III, for all Commerce bureaus and the Office of the Secretary.

An information security manager under the direction of the Office of the CIO is tasked with carrying out the responsibilities of the security program. These responsibilities, which are clearly defined in department policy, include developing security policies, procedures, and guidance and ensuring security oversight through reviews, which include tracking the implementation of required security controls.

Commerce lacks an effective centralized function to facilitate the integrated management of the security of its information system infrastructure. At the time of our review, the CIO, who had no specific budget to fulfill security responsibilities and exercised no direct control over the IT budgets of the Commerce bureaus, stated that he believed that he did not have sufficient resources or the authority to implement the department information security program. Until February 2000, when additional staff positions were established to support the information security manager's responsibilities, the information security manager had no staff to discharge these tasks. As of April 2001, the information security program was supported by a staff of three.

Commerce policy also requires each of its bureaus to implement an information security program that includes a full range of security responsibilities. These include appointing a bureauwide information security officer as well as security officers for each of the bureau's systems.

However, the Commerce bureaus we reviewed also lack their own centralized functions to coordinate bureau security programs with departmental policies and procedures and to implement effective programs for the security of the bureaus' information systems infrastructure. For example, four bureaus had staff assigned to security roles on a part-time basis and whose security responsibilities were treated as collateral duties.

In view of the widespread interconnectivity of Commerce's systems, the lack of a centralized approach to the management of security is particularly risky since there is no coordinated effort to ensure that minimal security controls are implemented and effective across the department. As demonstrated by our testing, intruders who succeeded in gaining access to a system in a bureau with weak network security could then circumvent the stronger network security of other bureaus. It is, therefore, unlikely that the security posture of the department as a whole will significantly improve until a more integrated security management approach is adopted and sufficient resources allotted to implement and enforce essential security measures departmentwide.

Risks Are Not Assessed

As outlined in our 1998 Executive Guide, understanding the risks associated with information security is the second key element of the information security management cycle. Identifying and assessing information security risks help to determine what controls are needed and what level of resources should be expended on controls. Federal guidance requires all federal agencies to develop comprehensive information security programs based on assessing and managing risks.[26] Commerce policy regarding information security requires (1) all bureaus to establish and implement a risk management process for all IT resources and (2) system owners to conduct a periodic risk analysis for all sensitive systems within each bureau.

Commerce bureaus we reviewed are not conducting risk assessments for their sensitive systems as required. Only 3 of the bureaus' 94 systems we reviewed[27] had documented risk assessments, one of which was still in draft. Consequently, most of the bureaus' systems are being operated without consideration of the risks associated with their immediate environment.

Moreover, these bureaus are not considering risks outside their immediate environment that affect the security of their systems, such as network interconnections with other systems. Although OMB Circular A-130, Appendix III, specifically requires that the risks of connecting to other systems be considered prior to doing so, several bureau officials acknowledged that they had not considered how vulnerabilities in systems that interconnected with theirs could undermine the security of their own systems. Rather, the initial decision to interconnect should have been made by management based on an assessment of the risk involved, the controls in place to mitigate the risk, and the predetermined acceptable level of risk. The widespread lack of risk assessments, as evidenced by the serious access control weaknesses revealed during our testing, indicates that Commerce is doing little to understand and manage risks to its systems.

---

[26]The February 1996 revision to OMB Circular A-130, Appendix III, *Security of Federal Automated Information Resources,* requires agencies to use a risk-based approach to determine adequate security, including a consideration of the major factors in risk management: the value of the system or application, threats, vulnerabilities, and the effectiveness of current or proposed safeguards. Additional guidance on effective risk assessment is available in NIST publications and in our *Information Security Risk Assessment: Practices of Leading Organizations* (GAO/AIMD-00-33).

[27]For purposes of reviewing Commerce's information security management program, we identified these 94 sensitive systems in the seven bureaus based on our discussions with bureau officials. We also included systems from an inventory of the bureaus' most critical systems that had been prepared by a contractor as part of an assessment of Commerce's Critical Infrastructure Protection Plan as well as from an inventory of critical systems compiled by the department in preparing for their Y2K remediation efforts.

Security Plans Are Not Prepared

Once risks have been assessed, OMB Circular A-130, Appendix III, requires agencies to document plans to mitigate these risks through system security plans. These plans should contain an overview of a system's security requirements; describe the technical controls planned or in place for meeting those requirements; include rules that delineate the responsibilities of managers and individuals who access the system; and outline training needs, personnel controls, and continuity plans. In summary, security plans should be updated regularly to reflect significant changes to the system as well as the rapidly changing technical environment and document that all aspects of security for a system have been fully considered, including management, technical, and operational controls.

None of the bureaus we reviewed had security plans for all of their sensitive systems. Of the 94 sensitive systems we reviewed, 87 had no security plans. Of the seven systems that did have security plans, none had been approved by management. Moreover, five of these seven plans did not include all the elements required by OMB Circular A-130, Appendix III. Without comprehensive security plans, the bureaus have no assurance that all aspects of security have been considered in determining the security requirements of the system and that adequate protection has been provided to meet those requirements.

Systems Are Not Authorized

OMB also requires management officials to formally authorize the use of a system before it becomes operational, when a significant change occurs, and at least every 3 years thereafter.[28] Authorization provides quality control in that it forces managers and technical staff to find the best fit for security, given technical constraints, operational constraints, and mission requirements. By formally authorizing a system for operational use, a manager accepts responsibility for the risks associated with it. Since the security plan establishes the system protection requirements and documents the security controls in place, it should form the basis for management's decision to authorize processing.

As of March 2001, Commerce management had not authorized any of the 94 sensitive systems that we identified. According to the more comprehensive data collected by the Office of the CIO in March 2000, 92 percent of all the department's sensitive systems had not been formally authorized. The lack of authorization indicates that systems' managers had

---

[28]Authorization is sometimes referred to as "accreditation."

not reviewed and accepted responsibility for the adequacy of the security controls implemented on their systems. As a result, Commerce has no assurance that these systems are being adequately protected.

Needed Policies Have Not Been Established

The third key element of computer security management, as identified during our study of information security management practices at leading organizations, is establishing and implementing policies. Security policies are important because they are the primary mechanism by which management communicates its goals and requirements. Federal guidelines require agencies to frequently update their information security policies in order to assess and counter rapidly evolving threats and vulnerabilities.

Commerce's information security policies are significantly outdated and incomplete. Developed in 1993 and partially revised in 1995, the department's information security policies and procedures manual, *Information Technology Management Handbook*, Chapter 10, "Information Technology Security," and attachment, "Information Technology Security" does not comply with OMB's February 1996 revision to Circular A-130, Appendix III, and does not incorporate more recent NIST guidelines. For example, Commerce's information security policy does not reflect current federal requirements for managing computer security risk on a continuing basis, authorizing processing, providing security awareness training, or performing system reviews. Moreover, because the policy was written before the explosive growth of the Internet and Commerce's extensive use of it, policies related to the risks of current Internet usage are omitted. For example, Commerce has no departmentwide security policies on World Wide Web sites, e-mail, or networking.

Further, Commerce has no departmental policies establishing baseline security requirements for all systems. For example, there is no departmental policy specifying required attributes for passwords, such as minimum length and the inclusion of special characters. Consequently, security settings differ both among bureaus and from system to system within the same bureau. Furthermore, Commerce lacks consistent policies establishing a standard minimum set of access controls. Having these baseline agencywide policies could eliminate many of the vulnerabilities discovered by our testing, such as configurations that provided users with excessive access to critical system files and sensitive data and expose excessive system information, all of which facilitate intrusions.

The Director of the Office of Information Policy, Planning, and Review and the Information Security Manager stated that Commerce management recognizes the need to update the department information security policy and will begin updating the security sections of the Information Technology Management Handbook in the immediate future.

Security Awareness and Training Are Not Adequately Promoted

The fourth key element of the security management cycle involves promoting awareness and conducting required training so that users understand the risks and the related policies and controls in place to mitigate them. Computer intrusions and security breakdowns often occur because computer users fail to take appropriate security measures. For this reason, it is vital that employees who use computer systems in their day-to-day operations are aware of the importance and sensitivity of the information they handle, as well as the business and legal reasons for maintaining its confidentiality, integrity, and availability.

OMB Circular A-130, Appendix III, requires that employees be trained on how to fulfill their security responsibilities before being allowed access to sensitive systems. The Computer Security Act mandates that all federal employees and contractors who are involved with the management, use, or operation of federal computer systems be provided periodic training in information security awareness and accepted information security practice. Specific training requirements are outlined in NIST guidelines,[29] which establish a mandatory baseline of training in security concepts and procedures and define additional structured training requirements for personnel with security-sensitive responsibilities.

Overall, none of the seven bureaus had documented computer security training procedures and only one of the bureaus had documented its policy for such training. This bureau also used a network user responsibility agreement, which requires that all network users read and sign a one-page agreement describing the network rules. Officials at another bureau stated that they were developing a security awareness policy document.

Although each of the seven bureaus had informal programs in place, such as a brief overview as part of the one-time general security orientation for new employees, these programs do not meet the requirements of OMB, the Computer Security Act, or NIST Special Publication 800-16. Such brief

---

[29]*Information Technology Security Training Requirements: A Role- and Performance-Based Model* (NIST Special Publication 800-16, April 1998).

overviews do not ensure that security risks and responsibilities are understood by all managers, users, and system administrators and operators. Shortcomings in the bureaus' security awareness and training activities are illustrated by the following examples.

- Officials at one bureau told us that they did not see training as an integral part of its security program, and provided an instructional handbook only to users of a specific bureau application.
- Another bureau used a generic computer-based training course distributed by the Department of Defense that described general computer security concepts but was not specific to Commerce's computing environment. Also, this bureau did not maintain records to document who had participated.
- Another bureau had limited awareness practices in place, such as distributing a newsletter to staff, but had no regular training program. Officials at this bureau told us that they were in the process of assessing its training requirements.

Only one Commerce bureau that we reviewed provided periodic refresher training. In addition, staff directly responsible for information security do not receive more extensive training than overviews since security is not considered to be a full-time function requiring special skills and knowledge. Several of the computer security weaknesses we discuss in this report indicate that Commerce employees are either unaware of or insensitive to the need for important information system controls.

Policies and Controls Are Not Monitored

The final key element of the security management cycle is an ongoing program of tests and evaluations to ensure that systems are in compliance with policies and that policies and controls are both appropriate and effective. This type of oversight is a fundamental element because it demonstrates management's commitment to the security program, reminds employees of their roles and responsibilities, and identifies and corrects areas of noncompliance and ineffectiveness. For these reasons, OMB Circular A-130, Appendix III, directs that the security controls of major information systems be independently reviewed or audited at least every 3 years. Commerce policy also requires information security program oversight and tasks the program manager with performing compliance reviews of the bureaus as well as verification reviews of individual systems. The government information security reform provisions of the fiscal year 2001 National Defense Authorization Act require annual independent reviews of IT security in fiscal years 2001 and 2002.

No oversight reviews of the Commerce bureaus' systems have been performed by the staff of Commerce's departmentwide information security program. The information security manager stated that he was not given the resources to perform these functions. Furthermore, the bureaus we reviewed do not monitor the effectiveness of their information security. Only one of the bureaus has performed isolated tests of its systems. In lieu of independent reviews, in May 2000, the Office of the CIO, using a draft of the CIO Council's Security Assessment Framework, requested that all Commerce bureaus submit a self-assessment of the security of their systems based on the existence of risk assessments, security plans, system authorizations, awareness and training programs, service continuity plans, and incident response capabilities. This self-assessment did not require testing or evaluating whether systems were in compliance with policies or the effectiveness of implemented controls. Nevertheless, the Office of the CIO's analysis of the self-assessments showed that 92 percent of Commerce's sensitive systems did not comply with federal security requirements. Specifically, 63 percent of Commerce's systems did not have security plans that comply with federal guidelines, 73 percent had no risk assessments, 64 percent did not have recovery plans, and 92 percent had not been authorized for operational use.

The information security manager further stated that, because of the continued lack of resources, the Office of the CIO would not be able to test and evaluate the effectiveness of Commerce's information security controls to comply with the government information security reform provisions requirement of the fiscal year 2001 National Defense Authorization Act. Instead, the information security manager stated that he would ask the bureaus to do another self-assessment. In future years, the information security manager intends to perform hands-on reviews as resources permit.

Conclusions

The significant and pervasive weaknesses that we discovered in the seven Commerce bureaus we tested place the data and operations of these bureaus at serious risk. Sensitive economic, personnel, financial, and business confidential information is exposed, allowing potential intruders to read, copy, modify, or delete these data. Moreover, critical operations could effectively cease in the event of accidental or malicious service disruptions.

Poor detection and response capabilities exacerbate the bureaus' vulnerability to intrusions. As demonstrated during our own testing, the bureaus' general inability to notice our activities increases the likelihood that intrusions will not be detected in time to prevent or minimize damage.

These weaknesses are attributable to the lack of an effective information security program, that is, lack of centralized management, a risk-based approach, up-to-date security policies, security awareness and training, and continuous monitoring of the bureaus' compliance with established policies and the effectiveness of implemented controls. These weaknesses are exacerbated by Commerce's highly interconnected computing environment in which the vulnerabilities of individual systems affect the security of systems in the entire department, since a compromise in a single poorly secured system can undermine the security of the multiple systems that connect to it.

Recommendations for Executive Action

We recommend that the Secretary direct the Office of the CIO and the bureaus to develop and implement an action plan for strengthening access controls for the department's sensitive systems commensurate with the risk and magnitude of the harm resulting from the loss, misuse, or modification of information resulting from unauthorized access. Targeted timeframes for addressing individual systems should be determined by their order of criticality. This will require ongoing cooperative efforts between the Office of the CIO and the Commerce bureaus' CIOs and their staff. Specifically, this action plan should address the logical access control weaknesses that are summarized in this report and will be detailed, along with corresponding recommendations, in a separate report designated for "Limited Official Use." These weaknesses include

- password management controls,
- operating system controls, and
- network controls.

We recommend that the Secretary direct the Office of the CIO and the Commerce bureaus to establish policies to identify and segregate incompatible duties and to implement controls, such as reviewing access activity, to mitigate the risks associated with the same staff performing these incompatible duties.

We recommend that the Secretary direct the Office of the CIO and the Commerce bureaus to establish policies and procedures for authorizing, testing, reviewing, and documenting software changes prior to implementation.

We recommend that the Secretary direct the Office of the CIO to require the Commerce bureaus to develop and test, at least annually, comprehensive recovery plans for all sensitive systems.

We recommend that the Secretary direct the Office of the CIO to establish a departmentwide incident handling function with formal procedures for preparing for, detecting, responding to, and reporting incidents.

We recommend that the Secretary direct the Office of the CIO and the Commerce bureaus to develop intrusion detection and incident response capabilities that include

- installing updates to system software with known vulnerabilities,
- installing warning banners on all network access paths,
- installing intrusion detection systems on networks and sensitive systems, and
- implementing policies and procedures for monitoring log files and audit trails on a regular schedule commensurate with risks for potentially unauthorized access to computer resources.

We recommend that the Secretary direct the Office of the CIO to develop and implement an effective departmentwide security program. Such a program should include establishing a central information security function to manage an ongoing cycle of the following security activities:

- Assessing risks and evaluating needs, which include

  - developing security plans for all sensitive systems that comply with federal guidelines as outlined in OMB A-130, Appendix III, and NIST SP 800-18 and
  - formally authorizing all systems before they become operational, upon significant change, and at least every 3 years thereafter.

- Updating the information security program policies to

  - comply with current federal regulations regarding risk assessments, specific security controls that must be included in security plans, management authorization to process, audits and reviews, security incidents, awareness and training, and contingency planning,
  - address vulnerabilities associated with Commerce's widespread use of Internet technologies, and

- provide minimum baseline standards for access controls to all networked systems to reduce risk in Commerce's highly interconnected environment.

- Developing and implementing a computer security awareness and training program.

- Developing and implementing a management oversight process that includes periodic compliance reviews and tests of the effectiveness of implemented controls. This process should include audits and reviews and establish clear roles, responsibilities, and procedures for tracking identified vulnerabilities and ensuring their remediation.

We also recommend that the Secretary of Commerce, the Office of the CIO, and the bureau CIOs direct the appropriate resources and authority to fulfill the security responsibilities that Commerce policy and directives task them with performing and to implement these recommendations.

In addition, we recommend that the Secretary take advantage of the opportunity that the installation of the new network infrastructure will provide to improve security. Specifically, by establishing strong departmental control over the network, Commerce could require all bureaus using this common network to meet a minimum level of security standards. This would help to ensure that weaknesses in one bureau's security will not undermine the security of all interconnecting bureaus, as is now the case.

Agency Comments

In providing written comments on a draft of this report, which are reprinted in appendix II, the Secretary of Commerce concurred with our findings and stated that Commerce is committed to improving the information security posture of the department. According to the Secretary, the bureaus we reviewed have developed and are currently implementing action plans to correct the specific problems we identified. He further stated that the heads of the Commerce bureaus have been directed to give priority to information security and to allocate sufficient resources to ensure that adequate security is in place. Moreover, the Secretary of Commerce said that he had approved an IT management restructuring plan on June 13, 2001, that would give the department CIO, as well as the bureau CIOs, new authority to strengthen the departmentwide information security program. He further stated that on July 23, 2001, he had established a task force on information security to develop a comprehensive and effective program for the department.

As agreed with your office, unless you publicly announce the contents of this report earlier, we will not distribute it until 10 days from the date of this letter. At that time, we will send copies to the Ranking Minority Member of the Committee; the Chairmen and Ranking Minority Members of the Senate Committee on Governmental Affairs; Senate Committee on Commerce, Science, and Transportation; and House Committee on Government Reform; as well as to other interested members of the Congress. We will also send copies to the Honorable Johnnie E. Frazier, Inspector General, Department of Commerce, and the Honorable Mitchell E. Daniels, Jr., Director, Office of Management and Budget.

If you have any questions regarding this report, please contact me at (202) 512-3317 or Elizabeth Johnston, Assistant Director, at (202) 512-6345. We can also be reached by e-mail at daceyr@gao.gov and johnstone@gao.gov respectively. Key contributors to this report are listed in appendix IV.

Sincerely yours,

Robert F. Dacey
Director, Information Security Issues

Appendix I: Objectives, Scope, and Methodology

Our objectives were to determine if the Department of Commerce has effectively implemented (1) logical access and other information system controls over its computerized data, (2) incident detection and response capabilities, and (3) an effective information security management program and related procedures. To accomplish these objectives, we applied appropriate sections of our Federal Information System Controls Audit Manual (GAO/AIMD-12.19.6), which describes our methodology for reviewing information system controls that affect the integrity, confidentiality, and availability of computerized data associated with federal agency operations.

As requested by the committee, the scope of our review was focused on seven Commerce bureaus: the Bureau of Export Administration, the Economic Development Administration, the Economics and Statistics Administration, the International Trade Administration, the Minority Business Development Agency, the National Telecommunications and Information Administration, and the Office of the Secretary. All of these bureaus are based at the Hoover Building in Washington, DC and have missions related to or support for trade development, reporting, assistance, regulation, and oversight.

In reviewing key logical access controls over Commerce's computerized data, we included in the scope of our testing systems that Commerce defined as critical to the mission of the department in that their disruption would jeopardize the national interest or national requirements relating to securing the U.S. economy, national security, and the delivery of essential private sector services. We also included systems that fit OMB Circular A-130, Appendix III's criteria for requiring special protection, i.e. general support systems, such as local area networks, and major applications. In addition, we included (1) applications that support the department and are important for the operations of the Office of the Secretary and (2) important web servers that support the missions of the bureaus.

We examined the configuration and control implementation for each of the computer operating system platforms and for each of the bureaus' computer networks that support these bureaus' mission-critical operations. In total, we assessed 120 systems, including 8 firewalls, 20 routers, 15 switches, and over 50 other network support or infrastructure devices.

We conducted penetration tests of Commerce's systems from both inside the Hoover building using an internal Commerce address and from a remote location through the Internet. We attempted to penetrate

Commerce's systems and exploit identified control weaknesses to verify the vulnerability they presented. We also met with Commerce officials to discuss possible reasons for vulnerabilities we identified and the department's plans for improvement.

To evaluate incident detection and response capabilities, we focused on Commerce's ability to prevent, detect, respond to, and report incidents. We examined whether Commerce bureaus (1) installed the latest system software patches, warning banners, and intrusion detection systems to deter intruders, (2) activated and reviewed access logs to ensure that incidents were detected, (3) implemented procedures to ensure that bureaus responded to incidents in an appropriate manner, and (4) generated and reviewed incident reports.

To review security program management and related procedures, we reviewed pertinent departmentwide policies, guidance, and security plans for each of the bureaus' sensitive systems and held discussions with officials responsible for developing and implementing these policies and plans throughout Commerce. This included

- analyzing departmentwide and bureau policies to determine (1) their compliance with OMB and NIST guidance and (2) whether they incorporated the management best practices identified in our executive guide *Information Security Management: Learning From Leading Organizations* (GAO/AIMD-98-68, May 1998);
- meeting with officials in Commerce's Office of the Chief Information Officer, which is responsible for managing Commerce's information security program, to determine what actions Commerce has taken to ensure effective security program implementation;
- discussing security plan development and implementation with officials in Commerce's Office of the Chief Information Officer and the seven bureaus; and
- reviewing system security plans from the seven bureaus to determine if they complied with Commerce's departmentwide policies and OMB and NIST guidance.

We performed our audit work from August 2000 through May 2001 in accordance with generally accepted government auditing standards. Because our work was focused on performing tests of selected computer-based security controls, we did not fully evaluate all computer controls. Consequently, additional vulnerabilities could exist that we did not identify.

Appendix II: Comments From the Department of Commerce

THE SECRETARY OF COMMERCE
Washington, D.C. 20230

JUL 3 0 2001

Mr. Robert Dacey
Director, Information Security Issues
General Accounting Office
Washington, D.C. 20548

Dear Mr. Dacey:

Thank you for the opportunity to comment on the draft GAO report entitled Information Security: Weaknesses Place Commerce Data and Operations At Serious Risk (GAO-02-751). This report documents a GAO review of seven Commerce organizations. The review has substantiated both specific weaknesses associated with the information systems of these Commerce organizations, as well as a lack of an effective Department-wide information security program.

Because much of the work of the Department of Commerce on behalf of our citizens is reliant, directly or indirectly, on the quality and integrity of our data and information technology (IT) systems, we are committed to assuring that our data and IT systems are adequately protected against risks of loss, misuse, or unauthorized access. IT security is a priority for this Department. The heads of our Commerce bureaus have been directed to give their personal attention to this priority, and will allocate sufficient resources to make sure adequate security is in place. In strengthening the Commerce IT Security Program, the Department will have the benefit of the new authority given to the Department Chief Information Officer (CIO) and to the CIO's of the Commerce bureaus through the IT management restructuring plan I recently approved.

The Commerce bureaus that were reviewed by GAO have acted over the past several months to correct in a timely way the specific problems identified. The Department has already developed Corrective Action Plans and they are being implemented. On July 23, I established a Commerce Task Force on IT Security to develop an comprehensive and effective IT Security Program for the Department.

The Department of Commerce is aware of the fact that this is a serious problem, and we are committed to improving the IT security posture of the Department.

Warm regards,

Donald L. Evans

Appendix III: Overview of the Office of the Secretary and the Six Department of Commerce Bureaus Reviewed

Office of the Secretary

The Office of the Secretary (O/S) is the department's general management arm and provides the principal support to the Secretary in formulating policy and providing advice to the President. O/S provides program leadership for the department's functions and exercises general oversight of its operating agencies. This office includes subordinate offices that have departmentwide responsibilities or perform special program functions directly on behalf of the Secretary.

Bureau of Export Administration

The Bureau of Export Administration (BXA) is primarily responsible for administering and enforcing the nation's system for controlling exports of sensitive dual-use goods and technologies in accordance with the Export Administration Act and regulations. BXA's major functions include formulating and implementing export control policy; processing export license applications; conducting various policy, technical, and economic analyses; promulgating regulations; conducting industry outreach; and enforcing the Export Administration Act and regulations.

Economics and Statistics Administration

The Economics and Statistics Administration (ESA) produces, analyzes, and disseminates some of the nation's most important economic and demographic data. Important economic indicators produced by ESA include retail sales, housing starts and foreign trade. ESA houses the Economic Bulletin Board, a dial-up bulletin board system which delivers major U.S. government economic indicators from the Bureau of the Census, the Bureau of Economic Analysis, the Federal Reserve Board and the Labor Department. ESA issues federal export information and international economic data of interest to business, policy makers and researchers. ESA also provides the public with STAT-USA/Internet, an online resource updated daily that offers both domestic U.S. economic information and foreign trade information.

Economic Development Administration

The Economic Development Administration (EDA) provides grants to economically distressed communities to generate new employment, help retain existing jobs, and stimulate industrial and commercial growth. EDA programs help fund the construction of public works and development facilities, and are intended to promote industrial and commercial growth.

Appendix III: Overview of the Office of the
Secretary and the Six Department of
Commerce Bureaus Reviewed

One EDA program is designed to help states and local areas design and implement strategies for adjusting to changes that cause or threaten to cause serious economic damage. Another program awards grants and cooperative agreements for studies designed to increase knowledge about emerging economic development issues, determine the causes of economic distress, and locate ways to alleviate barriers to economic development. Twelve Trade Adjustment Assistance Centers around the country receive funds to provide technical assistance to certified businesses hurt by increased imports.

International Trade Administration

The International Trade Administration (ITA) is responsible for promoting U.S. exports of manufactured goods, nonagricultural commodities, and services and associated trade policy issues. ITA works closely with U.S. businesses and other government agencies, including the Office of the U.S. Trade Representative and the Department of Treasury. Through its Market Access and Compliance Unit, ITA formulates and implements international economic policies to obtain market access for American firms and workers as well as compliance by foreign nations with U.S. international trade agreements. ITA also advises on international trade and investment policies pertaining to U.S. industrial sectors, carries out programs to strengthen domestic export competitiveness, and promotes U.S. industry's increased participation in international markets. Through its Import Administration, it administers legislation that counters unfair foreign trade practices. Finally, ITA's U.S. & Foreign Commercial Service, which has 105 domestic offices and 157 overseas posts in 84 countries, promotes the exports of U.S. companies and helps small and medium-sized businesses market their goods and services abroad.

Minority Business Development Agency

The Minority Business Development Agency's (MBDA) mission is to promote growth and competitiveness of the nation's minority-owned and operated businesses. MBDA seeks to improve minority business enterprise access to domestic and international marketplaces and improved opportunities in financing for business startup and expansion. MBDA provides management and technical assistance to minority individuals who own or are trying to establish a business through a network of business development centers in areas with large concentrations of minority populations and businesses. This includes assistance with planning, bidding, estimating, bonding, construction, financing, procurement, international trade matters, franchising, accounting, and

Appendix III: Overview of the Office of the
Secretary and the Six Department of
Commerce Bureaus Reviewed

marketing. MBDA has agreements with banks and other lending institutions that are intended to help minority entrepreneurs gain access to capitol for business expansion or development purposes.

National Telecommunications and Information Administration

The National Telecommunications and Information Administration (NTIA) serves as the President's principal adviser on domestic and international communications and information policies pertaining to the nation's economic and technological advancement and to regulation of the telecommunications industry. In this respect, NTIA develops and presents U.S. plans and policies at international communications conferences and related meetings, coordinates U.S. government position on communication with federal agencies, and prescribes policies that ensure effective and efficient federal use of the electromagnetic spectrum. NTIA's program activities are designed to assist the Administration, the Congress, and regulatory agencies in addressing diverse technical and policy questions.

Appendix IV: GAO Staff Acknowledgments

Key contributors to this assignment were Edward Alexander, Gerald Barnes, Lon Chin, West Coile, Debra Conner, Nancy DeFrancesco, Denise Fitzpatrick, Edward Glagola, David Hayes, Brian Howe, Sharon Kittrell, Harold Lewis, Suzanne Lightman, Duc Ngo, Tracy Pierson, Kevin Secrest, Eugene Stevens, and William Wadsworth.